COOL
Special Effects

How to Stage Your Very Own Show

Karen Latchana Kenney

Consulting Editor, Diane Craig, M.A./Reading Specialist

ABDO
Publishing Company

Note to Adult Helpers

To complete the activities in this book, kids will need some supervision, especially when they are using utility knives, ladders and paint. Remind kids that they need an adult to help them with these activities. Likewise, if kids are scrounging around for materials, remind them to get permission from an adult before they use anything.

Before beginning, find a good place for kids to work. Make sure there is a specific cutting area with padding underneath. Protect surfaces with newspaper or an old sheet. When painting, find a space that is well ventilated and make sure kids protect their clothing.

If kids want to purchase materials, help them set a budget. Remind them that they also need to clean up after making their projects. And, finally, don't forget to encourage kids as they create their special effects!

Visit us at www.abdopublishing.com

Published by ABDO Publishing Company, 8000 West 78th Street, Edina, Minnesota 55439. Copyright © 2010 by Abdo Consulting Group, Inc. International copyrights reserved in all countries. No part of this book may be reproduced in any form without written permission from the publisher. The Checkerboard Library™ is a trademark and logo of ABDO Publishing Company.

Printed in the United States.
Design and Production: Colleen Dolphin, Mighty Media, Inc.
Photo Credits: Colleen Dolphin, Shutterstock, iStockphoto (Zsolt Biczó, brave-carp, Achim Prill)
Series Editor: Katherine Hengel, Pam Price
Activity Production: Britney Haeg

The following manufacturers/names appearing in this book are trademarks: Office Depot® Posterboard, Pepperidge Farm® Goldfish® Crackers, Nabisco® Barnum's Animals® Crackers, Nabisco® Teddy Grahams®

Library of Congress Cataloging-in-Publication Data

Kenney, Karen Latchana.
  Cool special effects : how to stage your very own show / Karen Latchana Kenney.
    p. cm. -- (Cool performances)
  Includes index.
  ISBN 978-1-60453-719-2
  1. Stage-lighting--Juvenile literature. 2. Theaters--Sound effects--Juvenile literature. 3. Theaters--Special effects--Juvenile literature. I. Title.

PN2091.E4K46 2010
792.02'4--dc22
                          2009001753

Get the Picture!

There are many activities and how-to photos in this title. Each how-to photo has a color border around it, so match the border color to the appropriate activity step!

 activity step →

Contents

Creating Cool Performances.. 4

Light Effects 6

Sound Effects 8

Special Effects 10

Stage Kit... 12

Prompt Book 14

Glowing Gobos 16

Gleaming Gels.. 18

Black Light.. 20

Sounds Real!.. 22

Singing Glasses 26

Starry Night 28

Rolling Waves 29

Conclusion.. 30

Glossary 31

Web Sites 31

Index... 32

CREATING COOL PERFORMANCES

What's it all about?

Imagine putting on your very own show! Performing in front of an **audience** sounds fun, right? It is! You can pretend to be anything you want to be. Create an **illusion** for your audience using costumes, makeup, and props. Tell a story by acting out a script. Each book in this series introduces you to a different performance element. Put all the books together, and you'll be ready to put on a cool show!

You can create many kinds of shows. You can tell a funny story or a serious story. Put on a musical or a fairy tale. Creep out your audience with a monster or a ghost story. You can even be an alien on a strange planet!

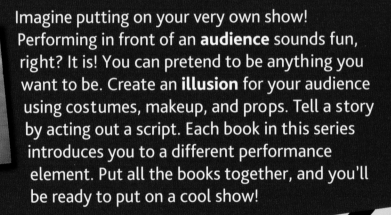

Cool Performances Series

Cool Costumes	Cool Scripts & Acting
Cool Makeup	Cool Sets & Props
Cool Productions	Cool Special Effects

Permission

Before beginning, find out if you have permission to put on a show. The activities in this book will require cutting, painting, and hanging. Get permission before you do these things! See if you have permission to spend money on materials. Set a budget!

Safety

- Make sure your work space has a window or door you can open for fresh air. This is important if you are using glue or paint. Wear utility gloves or an old shirt to protect your clothes and hands from glue or paint.
- Protect the floor by laying down some newspaper.
- Find an adult to help you if you will be using a utility knife, ladder, or electrical equipment.

Clean Up

- Put all your tools and materials away.
- Place lids on open containers.
- Wipe down the surfaces you worked on.
- Throw away unusable scraps.
- Store finished activities in an **appropriate** area.

Show Styles

There are many show styles. Shows can be one style or a combination of styles. Here are just a few.

Drama

Emotions are important in a drama. A dramatic show might be sad or it could make audiences laugh!

Fairy Tale

Fairy tales teach lessons. They have make-believe characters such as fairies, unicorns, and goblins.

Fantasy

Imaginary creatures make this kind of show fantastic! Mad scientists create monsters in laboratories, and aliens fly through space!

Musical

Singing is just as important as acting in a musical. Songs tell parts of the story.

LIGHT EFFECTS

See how lighting adds to a production

If it's too dark to see the show, you might as well go home! Stage lighting does more than just add light. It can create a certain mood or draw attention to an actor or a part of a set. Lighting helps tell the story in a show.

In a professional theater, stage lights usually hang on a **lighting rig** above the stage or the **audience**. A lighting designer decides where to place the lights and when to use them. A prompt book lets the crew know when to use each type of light during the show.

Spotlights direct the audience's attention to certain spots on the stage. Floodlights hang above the stage and light large areas.

Black Light
A black light is a lightbulb that gives off **ultraviolet** light. Black lights make certain surfaces glow.

Gel
A gel is a colored filter that is placed over a light. It changes the color the light projects.

Gobo
A gobo is a cutout placed over a light to project a picture or a pattern onto the stage.

Strobe Light
A strobe light quickly flashes on and off.

Spotlight Tips

Spotlights work best when you follow these tips:

- Make sure the space where you stage the show is very dark, both on stage and in the **house**.

- Spotlight an actor during a **monologue**, or long speech.

- Use the spotlight to hint that something is about to happen. For example, aim the spotlight at the door right before someone knocks on it.

SOUND EFFECTS

How the right sounds add to a story

Rumble and crack! When you hear the sound of thunder, you can imagine that there is a thunderstorm. If you hear creepy music, you might think the character on stage is a villain. Sound effects and music can take your show to another level. They can be used to hint at things that cannot be shown on stage. They can also express character qualities or say something about a specific scene.

A sound system is usually in place for big shows. This makes it possible for the **audience** to hear the actors, sound effects, and music. These systems include microphones, speakers, and a **soundboard**. A technical crew runs the sound system. Like the lighting crew, they use prompt books that tell them when to play music or sound effects. A homemade sound system could be as simple as a portable stereo with a microphone attachment.

A sound designer studies the script and decides how to use sound to add to the story. A honking car horn or the howl of wind are examples of sound effects. Sound effects can be recorded and played during a show. Or the sound can be made during the show. A prompt book will help the technical crew know when to play a certain sound.

Musical directors are in charge of live music or singing in the show. They instruct the musicians and decide which cast members will sing the songs. This is an important job in a musical.

SPECIAL EFFECTS

Making onstage illusions

You can use special effects to visually trick the **audience** into seeing something that is not really there.

Special effects can create a thick fog or blow a fierce wind on stage. In professional shows, these effects are created with special machines. Fog machines and dry ice can create fog or smoke on stage. Large fans are used to imitate wind. **Pyrotechnics** add fire and explosions. Actors seem to be able to fly when they are hooked up to special **harnesses** and ropes.

Professional special effects are often dangerous. Specially trained **technicians** run the machines. This protects the actors and audience. At home, you can create safe special effects. They may not look exactly like the real thing, but your audience will understand.

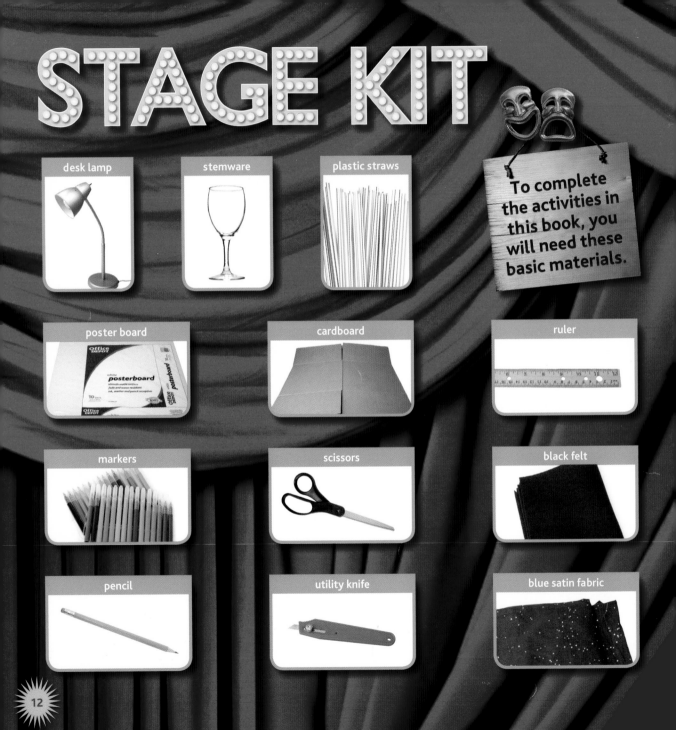

STAGE KIT

desk lamp

stemware

plastic straws

To complete the activities in this book, you will need these basic materials.

poster board

cardboard

ruler

markers

scissors

black felt

pencil

utility knife

blue satin fabric

12

black paint

empty foil bags

round, plastic containers

wood cutting board

paintbrushes

highlighters

nail

flashlight

notebook

colored cellophane

plastic tub

drinking glass

pushpins

black lightbulb

electrical tape

pitcher

hair comb

gravel

white twinkle lights

Prompt Book

Organize your lighting, sound, and special effects in a prompt book. Prompt books point out when and where effects take place based on the script.

STAGE KIT
- notebook
- copy of a script (optional)
- tape (optional)
- markers

Lights
- spotlight
- black light
- gel light (blue)

Sound
- clattering pots and pans
- lullaby music
- snoring

Special effects
- starry night
- wind

12

NARRATOR: And as Judy stretched out her hand toward the spinning wheel, a great and mighty wind began to brew around the castle. Then, as she touched the tip of the needle, and a drop of red blood dripped from her finger, the winds howled and terrible crashes echoed throughout the castle. (Judy freezes)

KING: (arms over head, running around, as pieces of stone begin to fall around him)
What is happening?! I must take cover!

NARRATOR: But as suddenly as the noise and winds and terrible crashes had begun, they suddenly stopped. And a peculiar quiet fell over all the castle. But what was happening?!

(King, Judy, and servants all start looking sleepy — rubbing their eyes, yawning, starting to fall over)

The castle was falling asleep! The whole castle had been cast under a powerful sleeping spell! But who had cast such a spell?

Open the notebook so that there is a blank page on the left and right sides.

Write the first page of your script on the right-hand page. If you have a copy of your script, tape the first page in the notebook instead.

Turn the page. Write or tape the next page of the script to the right-hand notebook page. Continue this process until you have the whole script in the notebook.

On each of the left-hand notebook pages, create three sections. Title the sections "Lights," "Sound," and "Special effects." Use a different color marker for each section.

Write each effect in the **appropriate** section. Then draw arrows to the places in the script where each effect should happen. Use this prompt book on the day of your big show to make sure each effect happens when it should!

Scene Stealers

To create your own script, check out the book *Cool Scripts & Acting*. You'll learn about dialogue, stage directions, and acting!

Glowing Gobos

A gobo projects shapes of light on stage. Gobos control light by blocking portions of a light's beam.

1. Cut out a 4 inch (10 cm) square of poster board.

2. Stand the flashlight on the poster board with the lens facedown. Trace around the end of the flashlight.

3. Draw the shape you want to project inside the outline of the flashlight. Ask an adult to help you cut out the shape with a utility knife. Use cardboard to protect your work surface. Throw away the cutout piece.

4. Paint one side of the remaining poster board with black paint. This will help block light.

5. Hold the poster board up to the flashlight. Make sure the black side is facing the light. Turn out the lights and shine the flashlight where you want the shape to appear. Try tilting the poster board or holding it farther away from the flashlight. This will change how the image appears!

Cool Gobo Shapes

Gleaming Gels

A gel is a thin, colored material that projects color. Place a gel in the path of a beam of light to create a special mood! Gels don't last forever. The light causes their color to fade over time.

STAGE KIT
- scissors
- ruler
- cardboard
- flashlight
- pencil
- utility knife
- tape
- black paint
- paintbrush
- colored cellophane

1. Cut out a 4 inch (10 cm) square of cardboard. Stand the flashlight on the cardboard with the lens facedown. Trace around the end of the flashlight.

2. Draw the shape you want to project inside the outline of the flashlight. Ask an adult to help you cut out the shape with a utility knife. Throw away the cutout piece.

3. Paint the remaining piece of cardboard black. Now cut out a piece of cellophane that is big enough to cover the circle.

4. Tape the cellophane to the black side of the cardboard. Do not let the tape show in the opening of the cardboard.

5. Shine your flashlight through the opening and point it at the stage.

Black Light

Control what an **audience** can see with black lights! Start with a dark stage, and then shine a black light. The **ultraviolet** light will cause some objects to glow in the dark!

Using highlighters, draw a design on an 11 × 14 inch (28 × 35.6 cm) piece of poster board.

Tape the poster board to the wall.

Put the black lightbulb into a utility lamp. Make sure the lightbulb is the correct wattage for the lamp.

Turn off all the lights. Aim the black light at the poster board and watch the design glow!

Make it Glow!

Black lights give off **ultraviolet** light. Any object that glows under ultraviolet light contains phosphor. A phosphor is a substance that converts ultraviolet light into visible light. This visible light is the glow that we see! White T-shirts and socks normally glow under a black light because many laundry detergents contain phosphors.

Sounds Real!

Add cool sounds to your show! Record sound effects ahead of time or create sound effects backstage during the performance. To make the sound effects seem real, make sure they match the onstage action. Watch the actors carefully and follow your prompt book.

STAGE KIT
- empty foil bags
- plastic tub
- gravel
- poster board
- round plastic containers
- wood cutting board
- drinking glass
- plastic straw
- hair comb

CRACKLING FIRE

Hold three or four empty foil bags in your hands and scrunch them together. It sounds like a crackling fire!

Footsteps on a Path

Pour gravel into a plastic tub. Step into the tub and walk in place.

Thunder

Grab a couple of big pieces of poster board. Wiggle them around quickly to create a sound like thunder.

GALLOPING HORSE

Place the wood cutting board in front of you. Hold a round, plastic container in each hand. Clomp the containers on the board one after the other. It sounds like a galloping horse!

BOILING WATER

Fill a drinking glass halfway with water and blow bubbles with a straw.

Telephone Voice

Speak into a glass. Change the angle of the glass until your voice sounds like it is coming through a telephone.

Crickets

Hold a comb with the teeth pointing out. Run your fingernail along the teeth. It sounds like crickets chirping!

Singing Glasses

In this activity, you will make music with **stemware**! The amount of water in each glass will determine the **pitch** of the sound.

STAGE KIT

- crystal stemware with thin edges
- pitcher full of water

1 Line up several glasses on a table. Put a different amount of water in each glass.

2 Wet your finger. Rub the rim of one of the glasses. Keep rubbing in a circle until you hear a whistling noise.

3 Now try out the other glasses to hear what sounds they make. If you can, rub two glasses at the same time. Create an **eerie** song!

Record It!

Think about the kinds of sounds that would work well in your show. Perhaps a creaky door, a telephone ringing, or clattering pots? Look around for things that you could use to create those sounds.

When you get your sounds just right, record them onto a cassette! Record the sounds in the order that you will use them in your show. Write down the order of your sounds. This will help you during the show!

Found Sounds

Many libraries have soundtracks and other sound effects on CDs. Visit your local library and check out their audio selections. You'll find recordings of cool sounds that you can't make at home!

Starry Night

This effect calls for twinkle lights. Make sure you tape the electrical cord to the ground so no one trips! Also, don't forget to turn the lights off when you aren't using them.

STAGE KIT

- black felt (enough to cover the back wall of your stage)
- large piece of cardboard
- nail
- white twinkle lights
- black electrical tape
- pushpins

1 Lay the black felt on the cardboard. Use a nail to randomly poke holes throughout the whole piece of felt. Or poke holes in the shape of a **constellation**!

2 Push the twinkle lights through the holes. Use black electrical tape to hold the lights in place. Use pushpins to secure the felt on the back wall of the stage. Plug in the twinkle lights and check out the stars!

Rolling Waves

Add water without the mess! This effect works great if an actor is pretending to swim across stage.

STAGE KIT
- blue satiny fabric (a little longer than the width of your stage)
- 2 people

1 Ask a friend to help you with this effect. Stand on opposite ends of the stage. Each of you should have one end of the fabric.

2 Flap the fabric up and down so that it makes waves.

CONCLUSION

Isn't it amazing what lighting, sounds, and special effects can add to a production? Special effects help create realistic **illusions** for your **audience**. Music and lighting can communicate a spooky, dramatic, or funny tone. When effects like these are used correctly, they highlight and enhance the story being performed.

But it takes more than cool special effects to put on a great production. Check out the other books in the Cool Performances series to learn more about putting on a show. Learn how to use makeup and costumes to create different looks. Practice your acting skills and try writing a script. Create unique sets and props. Then put everything together to make a great show. Have fun and let your imagination run wild!

GLOSSARY

appropriate – suitable, fitting, or proper for a specific occasion.

audience – a group of people watching a performance.

constellation – a group of stars that together form a pattern or shape.

eerie – strange and scary.

harness – strap used to keep a person safe.

house – the audience in a theater or concert hall.

illusion – something that looks real but is not.

lighting rig – a system that holds lights in a production.

monologue – a one-person speech in a production.

pitch – the highness or lowness of sound.

pyrotechnic – relating to fireworks.

soundboard – a machine that controls the sound in a production.

stemware – a glass with a thin stem and a flat base.

technician – a person who is skilled at a specific task.

ultraviolet – a type of light that cannot be seen with the human eye.

Web Sites

To learn more about putting on a show, visit ABDO Publishing Company on the World Wide Web at www.abdopublishing.com. Web sites about theater are featured on our Book Links page. These links are routinely monitored and updated to provide the most current information available.

INDEX

A

Adult supervision/permission, 2, 5, 17, 19

B

Black lights, 6, 20–21

Boiling water, creating sound of, 24

Buying materials, 2, 5

C

Cleaning up, 2, 5

Crickets, creating sound of, 25

D

Drama, as style of show, 5

F

Fairy tale, as style of show, 4, 5

Fantasy, as style of show, 5

Fire, creation of, 10, 22

Floodlights, 6

Fog, creation of, 10

Footsteps, creating sound of, 23

G

Gels, 6, 18–19

Glasses, creating music with, 26–27

Gobos, 6, 16–17

H

Horse, creating sound of, 24

I

Illusion, creation of, 4, 30

L

Light effects, 6–7, 16–17, 18–19, 20–21, 28

Lighting design/designers, 6

Lighting rig, 6

M

Materials. *See* Tools/Materials

Music, 9, 26–27

Musical, as style of show, 4, 5, 9

Musical directors, 9

P

Painting, 2, 5, 17, 19

Permission, asking for, 5. *See also* Adult supervision/permission

Prompt book, 6, 9, 14–15

Pyrotechnics, 10

R

Recording/Recordings, of sound effects, 9, 27

S

Safety concerns, 2, 5, 11

Script, and planning effects, 14–15

Shows, kinds/styles of, 4, 5

Singing, 9

Smoke, creation of, 10

Sound design/designers, 9

Sound effects, 8–9, 22–25, 26–27

Sound system, 9

Special effects, 10–11

Spotlights, 6, 7

Stage kit, 12–13. *See also* Tools/Materials

Stage lighting, 6. *See also* Light effects

Starry night, creation of, 28

Strobe light, 6

T

Telephone voice, creating sound of, 25

Thunder, creating sound of, 9, 23

Tools/Materials, for special effects, 2, 9, 12–13

U

Ultraviolet light, 20–21

Utility knife, 2, 5, 17, 19

W

Waves, creation of, 29

Wind, creating sound of, 9, 10

Work space, for creating special effects, 2, 5